Finding god
in
All Things

Brian Grogan S.J.

MESSENGER PUBLICATIONS

Published by
Messenger Publications,
37, Lower Leeson Street,
Dublin 2.
Tel: (01) 676 7491/2.
Fax: (01) 661 1606.

6 - 01 - 99G

ISBN 1 872245 48 X

05-0596

CONTENTS

Introduction

This little book originated as a series of articles in *The Sacred Heart Messenger* for 1995. Some minor changes have been necessary in order to accommodate the articles to this new format. Like Saint Ignatius and ourselves, the articles are on a pilgrimage in order to be more fully alive for a new situation. They began life as brave little pilgrims setting out alone, one month after the other, bumping into people and interacting with them and hopefully giving them new heart for the next phase of their journey. Now they are setting out on a new pilgrimage as a group bonded together. Please God they will make further friends along the way.

A few images occur to me which may help you as you begin to read: the first is of a tree-trunk and it comes from Ignatius; the second is the image of dancing; the third is of watching TV. Let us look at these in turn.

Tree-Trunk And Sculptor

There are very few persons who realise what God would make of them if they abandoned themselves entirely into his hands, and let themselves be formed by his grace.

A thick and shapeless tree-trunk would never believe that it could become a statue, admired as a miracle of sculpture, and would never submit itself to the chisel of the sculptor, who sees by his genius what he can make of it.

Many people who now scarcely live as Christians do not understand that they could become saints, if they would let themselves be formed by the grace of God and if they did not ruin his plans by resisting the work he wants to do.

This book is intended to help you to catch on to the wonder of yourself. At whatever stage of your journey you find yourself, you are being shaped and formed by God into the image of Jesus. This means becoming more and more open to God, until we possess God's fullness: further, it implies growing towards the fullness of love for humankind which Jesus had.

Dance

I met an accomplished dance teacher recently, who confided to me that his partners often told him how well he used to dance and how he would always ask them if they had enjoyed the experience. Invariably they said, 'Of course!' He knew that once the music had started and they had lost their initial self-consciousness they were caught up immediately in the dance. No longer passive, they brought their own personalities to it, each of them uniquely. He had the gift of sensing their individuality as it expressed itself in subtle ways, and was able to adjust effortlessly. 'You know,' he told me, 'the dance was in them somehow!'

God is a dancing God. God approaches us one by one and asks, 'May I have this dance?' God adjusts to our particular gifts and even if I am flat-footed, God brings it about that the dance is in me. It is important to notice that my dance with God is not an exclusive event removed from this world: rather, as we dance, God is signalling to me to invite other people in, because the divine dream is that God and all humankind will finally dance together.

Watching Television

My third image is of yourself as you watch the TV news. As a succession of dreadful and tragic events are unfolded, you begin to face the gnawing questions, *What is going on? Is there any hope for humankind?* It is when you begin to ponder on the state of our world and your own role in it, and whether God has abandoned humankind to its own devices, that Ignatian spirituality begins to have meaning for you. This is because its central focus is on the interaction between you, the real world around you, and God who labours in the world and seeks your help to bring human history to a happy conclusion.

Many people see the world as a religious desert, whereas Ignatius was convinced that it is the arena where the Spirit of God is joyously active and indefatigable. We are invited into the life of God, not simply to rest there but rather to share in the great enterprise of bringing the world to the fullness of God. Our gifts and resources are for others, just as the gifts and resources of others are meant to be for us, and all of these come from God.

Ignatius used often end his letters with a prayer that God would change us from being weak and sad to being strong and joyous. This is my prayer for you. Left to ourselves, and sensitive to the pain and tragedy of our world, we would rightly be weak and sad; but when we become aware that God is powerfully active in our world and is inviting us to play our part in it according to the gifts and abilities that we have, then we can begin to feel strong and joyous. We are with God and God is with us.

Chapter One

Finding God In All Things

The following pages offer an introduction to *Ignatian Spirituality*. Let me assure you immediately that I am not presenting a scholarly analysis which will demand great effort and concentration on your part. Rather, I am inviting you to get involved in something. Participating rather than spectating is what matters in dealing with the relationship between God, yourself and your world.

God Involved in Your Life

Why is this important? Because God is already totally involved in your life and you know something about that already. It is like an engagement - two people are in love: there is a promise, a dream, and a sense that to move to ever fuller commitment would be good for both.

These pages offer hints on how you can deepen your appreciation of what God is doing and what he desires for you. The ideas outlined here have value only insofar as they evoke an experience for you, open up a window into the mystery of the relationship between God and yourself. At the end of each chapter you will find an exercise which will help you to enter personally into some aspect of God's relationship with you.

What Is Spirituality?

The word 'spirituality' can be a real stumbling block! Don't spend too much time trying to define it, but think of it as 'relationship'. Relationship is a word that implies life; life between persons. Marriage and friendship cannot be defined, nor can our relationship with God, but what is implied is life between two persons. No words are big enough to capture the mystery of what goes on in a relationship; if this is true for marriage and friendship, how much more true when one of the partners is divine and the other partner is you?

Spirituality is concerned with the person in relation to God. It concerns our experience of God, not our experience of ideas, rules or obligations. What differentiates it from theology is its focus on the actual, living, moment by moment relationship between the person and God in real life situations. So we are back to the idea of relationship! This relationship is meant to be one of ever growing awareness of God's presence and involvement in each person's life. It covers the whole of life.

The shortest of all definitions of Ignatian spirituality is *'finding God in all things'*. This is also Ignatius' preferred statement of what his life was about. These chapters will try to tease out the vast richness encapsulated in this tiny phrase, and you are invited to ponder, reflect and pray over what strikes you in them. May they bring you many 'moments of glad grace' and help you know in a heartfelt way that truly God can be found in all things.

What Was Ignatius Like?

Ignatius of Loyola (1491-1556) was, first and foremost, a real person; he was enthusiastic, alive, warm and attractive, a visionary leader, capable and energetic. As his life moved on he slowly became more reflective about what was going on in himself. He became a man passionately in love with God and the world around him. He came to understand that this world of ours is in fact God's world and that God is busy in it and, therefore, can be found everywhere in it.

Historically Ignatius spans two worlds. Born at the end of the Medieval Period he lived out his life in the world of the Renaissance. As a young man he was shaped by the medieval traditions of knighthood and chivalry. Had God not dramatically intervened, by beckoning him in a different direction, he might have lived out the life of a conquistador, and would probably have died violently! For the mentality of Ignatius was that of the conquistadors.

Conquistadors

They were knights who were totally individual, completely themselves. There was nothing of the 'unknown soldier' about them: they had a passion for personal reputation and were full of prickly pride; they disliked discipline and regimentation, and insisted on being consulted about every decision. On the other hand, they were totally committed to the person whom they had chosen as their lord. This helps to explain their extravagant daring and their indifference to wounds, fatigue and even death. They conducted themselves with the high seriousness of men conscious of taking part in great deeds.

No wonder, then, that Ignatius was willing in 1521 to defend the town of Pamplona, single-handed if necessary, for the sake of his lord, the Duke of Najera. The same year saw the fall of Mexico City to Cortes, with a tiny army which kept together in spite of incredible hardships because of the personal bond between each soldier and his leader. Out of this period, then, Ignatius comes across as almost innocent, single-minded and totally committed, with a conviction of his own importance in the scheme of things and of the rightness of what he was doing.

Enter God

During the siege of Pamplona his leg was badly injured by a cannonball. He was then about thirty years old. He lay in bed for a long time while it healed. He liked to read and dream of adventure, but, unfortunately, there were no interesting novels or adventure stories to hand; the only books available to him during this time were the *Life of Christ* and the *Lives of the Saints.*

Reading these stories, he slowly began to dream a different dream. He pondered anew on the purpose of life and he found, to his surprise, that he was shifting his allegiance from an earthly to a heavenly lord. Listen to his own words: 'I was like a man roused from heavy slumber...What strange life is this that I am now beginning to live?' Others said of him that he became 'a new man with a new mind'. How did this happen?

Found God was On His Side

From reading the *Life of Christ* and the *Lives of the Saints* Ignatius came to see - with shock - that God loved him, and was personally interested in him. Being imaginative, Ignatius was able to enter fully into the scenes of the Gospel: he now saw Jesus as the true Lord, the one whose enterprise was most worthwhile, the one who had suffered and died and risen for him. He became aware that God was for him, on his side, and had been actively so always. Overwhelmed by this realisation, his initial response was one of gratitude. He wondered to himself: Why was God so good? But there was no answer. There *is* no answer. God is just like that.

It is consoling for us that thirty years of life had gone by for Ignatius before he stumbled on the mysterious encounters which the human heart has with God. Such encounters are intensely private and unwitnessed - and usually unrecorded. Yet we all have these encounters because God meets us in every situation. When Ignatius caught on to this he began to record his experiences. In his meetings with others he found it helpful to share something of how God dealt with him and how he himself dealt with God.

But everyone's life is totally unique, and Ignatius' gift lay primarily in his ability to enable others to enter a process of contemplation and reflection whereby they could meet God directly themselves and come to understand how God was engaging with them in their own life situations.

Thus were born the *Spiritual Exercises* of St Ignatius which are 'ways of introducing people to God and helping them to find God in their lives'.

Change of Direction

As a result of what he had experienced, Ignatius changed his lifestyle. The knight became the pilgrim, which is the title he gives himself in his *Autobiography*. He lived as a beggar and a hermit and tried to emulate the saints in a crude and untutored way. He had great desires to serve God but he had much to learn about how God wished to be served. Fully eighteen years went by before he saw that God was calling him to found a religious order. This order was to be a group of like-minded men fired with the desire of being totally at the service of God and humankind within the Church.

The last sixteen years of his life (1540-1556) were spent in a small room in Rome, administering the affairs of the newly born *Company of Jesus*, which became known as the Jesuits. He had moved from knight to pilgrim to founder and finally to administrator. Like many of us he found that life evolves in very unexpected ways.

The Key Issue

We know that Ignatius deeply desired to be directly involved in working for the good of others but we also know that he had learned to allow God take the initiative in shaping his life. In his *Autobiography*, dictated in the third person shortly before he died, we read that, 'his devotion always went on increasing, that is, the ease with which he found God, which was then greater than he had ever had in his life. Whenever he wished, at whatever hour, he could find God'. In whatever situation, dramatic or dull, finding God was for Ignatius the key issue, and so it is the perfect summary of Ignatian spirituality.

SUGGESTED EXERCISE

● Find a place that can be yours for a little while each day; seat yourself in a friendly chair, or maybe in a corner that you have not used before, or even in the garden or the park.

● Generally speaking, in the beginning it is good to fix the same time each day. Initially it can seem difficult to organise, but after a while it is surprising how you will find yourself looking forward to it. The anticipated meeting becomes precious.

● Make yourself comfortable; if you are indoors perhaps you might light a candle. Trust that God is there with you, that he has been waiting eagerly for you to come to talk. Perhaps you would like to talk to Jesus, like good friends hungry for a chat! Tell him how you are feeling. Tell him your own story, and listen to his.

● Reading the stories of Jesus' life, the Gospels, will help you get to know him better as a real living person.

● Select a passage from his life story. Read the piece you have chosen and then spend some time reflecting on the words or the message. Do as Ignatius did when he imagined himself in the stories. He wove himself into the fabric of Jesus' life on earth: he met Jesus and the disciples in their everyday lives. Try it now yourself! After all, the stories were written for you.

● Read John 1:38 and allow yourself to hear Jesus ask you the question, 'What do you want?' And then, answer Jesus. This is how a conversation begins and how two hearts become immersed in each other.

Chapter Two

You Are Important!

In the first chapter we talked about Ignatius' early life, in which he shows a deep awareness of his own importance. As a knight in armour, he believed that one person could make all the difference between victory and defeat. He had courage and that gave him freedom to risk everything for what he judged to be important. Somebody who lately stumbled on Ignatius said to me, 'I think Ignatius walked tall and free; when he saw what was to be done he swished his cloak and went and did it'!

Overwhelmed by Love

A recent study of the early companions of Ignatius reveals them as a group of persons who were convinced of what they were about, confident and happy. Why so? It is surely because with the help of Ignatius and the *Spiritual Exercises* they were overwhelmed by the realisation that the God of Jesus Christ was totally in love with them, totally for them, and that the only response to this was gratitude and a readiness to share this good news with others. These first exponents of Ignatian spirituality are described as engaged in a '*ministry of consolation*' which meant bringing others to a personal awareness of God's limitless love for them, and then inviting them to the intimacy which escorts it.

How About You?

Do you believe that you are important to God, *just as you are?* Unless you and I believe this, it is very difficult to get going and to have the freedom and courage to risk everything for God, as Ignatius did.

Is much of the passivity which lies heavily on the Church in our time due to the fact that we have picked up a contrary message? Ignatian spirituality maintains that we are first of all totally and passionately loved, that God relates to us as the great lover who 'gives and shares with the beloved what he possesses...and desires to give himself to me', as the Spiritual Exercises put it.

The message we seem to have picked up and live out of, is that we are first of all sinners, that we are loved out of pity, and that God cannot hope for very much from us. If we think this way, we believe that we are problems to God and problematic to ourselves, and so life is heavy and joyless, and without hope - except in the condescending mercy of God.

Wayward Beloved

There are two truths here which must be seen in right perspective to one another: firstly, we are loved; secondly, we are sinners. Scripture opens its account of our relationship to God by stating that God creates us in his own image and likeness, and sees that we are very good. Later comes the account of the fall, but the loving continues: humankind is constantly being called back into loving relationship. We are indeed called to repent, to be converted, and never to despair.

St Paul tells the Ephesians that they were chosen before the world began, to be holy and blameless in God's sight and to live through love in his presence. In his letter to the Romans (Chs 5 and 8) he underlines the fact that in spite of our failure to live up to the love shown us, the love goes steadily on: it is poured into our hearts, it overwhelms us; nothing can ever separate us from the love of God, and this is proved by the death and resurrection of Jesus.

Ignatius knew this: he knew what sinning was all about, and he refers frequently to the shame and horror he experienced as he became more fully aware of the fact that he was being loved in the middle of all his sinning. If he emerges as confident and happy after his conversion experience at Manresa in 1522, it is because he is aware of being lovingly sustained by God and of being welcomed into companionship with Jesus in his campaign for the establishment of a truly loving community of humankind.

God is Different

Ignatian spirituality, then, maintains that you are important to God and to God's world; that you have a role to play; that you have unique gifts and creativity; and so, that your role in the world will be uniquely yours.

We could spend a lifetime asking, 'Why am I important to God?' It can seem an honest question but it can hide a mistrust of the other's goodness and excuse us from the risk of engaging in the relationship. Whatever our bad experiences in human relationships we need to allow God to be different, to be the *One who can do nothing but love.*

'As emeralds are green, so God is love.' I am important to God because God chooses so. As a child, I was important to my parents. To ask them 'Why?' would be a wrong and hurtful question. It is simply so. Good friends are important to each other; husbands and wives are important to each other. For either to ask 'Why?' in a doubting way is to spoil the relationship. Love is the starting point and needs no justification.

Not Just 'Holy People'

Do we believe that the reason for our creation is that there are three divine persons at the heart of the world who love one another totally, and who love us into existence and want us to be happy with them forever? Even if we say 'Yes' to this question, the suspicion remains that God ends up by loving only 'holy people' or 'good people', and not sinners like ourselves.

Personal failings discourage us because we feel that God could not be with us in our mess. Serious day-to-day problems such as being in debt, watching a loved one suffering because of AIDS, or a beautiful teenager pregnant too soon, also discourage us because we feel that God couldn't understand. We worry about being a burden to God; we try to travel alone but we fail, and this creates more distance between God and ourselves.

'I Am With You!'

Ignatian spirituality tells us that we are not alone; that God is not removed from our world. The task is not so much about getting out of the mess in order to find God, but more, much more, about bringing God into the mess. God meets us in our personal experience, in our relationships, dreams, hopes, pains and worries. Two key elements in Ignatian spirituality interplay here. First, because we are important to God, our life experience is important as the place where God meets us. Second, God deals directly with us and it is by reflecting on our personal experience that we come to an awareness of what is really going on.

It is clear from what I have already said that Ignatian spirituality is intensely personal and intimate: it would be totally wrong, however, to interpret it as individualistic. The intense personal relationship between Jesus and his Father overflows into limitless love for all humankind. So it does for Ignatius and all other saints. Being important to God will involve being totally available for God's service in love of the world.

SUGGESTED EXERCISE

● 'Look, I am standing at the door, knocking. If you hear me calling and open the door, I will come in to share your meal, side by side with you' Revelation 3:20.

● Imagine a knock at the door. A train of events is set in motion; you become more alert, wondering who is there. Whatever is happening in the house stops for a moment and perhaps the dog barks or the cat wakes up. On your way to answer the knock you may tidy some papers that are strewn around, glance in the hall mirror perhaps. You are wondering, anticipating: Who can it be?

● On opening the door there is a definite change of feeling, a change of experience. If it is someone you know and love and if the visit is a surprise, it is such a good feeling. No matter what was going on in the house, space is made for the friend, an extra place is set at the table.

● Imagine opening the door and finding Jesus standing there, smiling, asking if he may come in...you ushering him in along the hall...setting an extra place at the table...chatting...sharing the food.

● At the end of such a meal you are changed, because Jesus and you have spent some time together. The conversation between you somehow alters the way you have been seeing things.

Chapter Three

What Is God Like?

If you were asked, 'What is God like?' how much would you have to say? Not very much, perhaps, because we find it so hard to talk about God. Yet in each of us there is a deep longing to know God. If you asked Ignatius of Loyola the same question, he would stop, smile, maybe shed tears - as he often did when he thought about God - and then begin to share with you something from his own long journey of growing in appreciation of God.

Ablaze with God

Ignatius was fully thirty-years-old before he became aware of God as the centre of his life. It was through reading *The Life of Christ* and the *Gospels* during his convalescence that he woke up to the astonishing fact that God was passionately interested in him, totally in love with him. In the intimacy of long contemplation, Ignatius grasped at a very deep level that the life, passion and resurrection of Jesus were all for him. Further, he came to understand that God was working on his behalf in every detail of his life.

Through all of this he struggled to the startling awareness that he must be important to God. This gave a whole new meaning to his life and choices. He became aware that

God was present in his experiences, that there was no dividing line between life and prayer, but that God was constantly speaking to him in his ordinary living: nudging, challenging, helping, beckoning, opening up new undreamt of vistas of love and service.

He became aware that God was accepting him as he was, and shaping him for his own loving purposes. In a brief phrase in his *Autobiography* he lets us in on what was happening between himself and God: he was becoming 'a generous spirit, ablaze with God'.

What God Is Not

Like ourselves, Ignatius had to work through narrow images of God to get to richer ones. He would have rejected the idea that God is a lonely celestial watchmaker who has wound up the universe and got it going, and who leaves it now to tick away and run down by itself. Likewise, he had to discard the picture of God as a wise and serious judge, or as an accountant with a frighteningly accurate memory and a red pen, who watches out for our mistakes.

Moving on to a deeper level, he would sympathise with our tendency to think of God as the interfering controller. Caught in this image, we find it so hard to take the risk of exposing our needs and our brokenness to God, because we do not trust that he is totally good and always on our side.

We struggle to keep him at a distance so that he won't see the darker side of ourselves which we know about but are reluctant to admit. Ignatius was aware of how we battle to make God fit in with our narrow plans, how we control, tame and 'neaten' God. But he would say to us that by operating out of this distorted image we limit God's loving and creative influence in our lives.

In trying to bring God under our control we remove the risk of being surprised by God. We opt for peace and security and a quiet life, and so everything becomes ordinary and pedestrian and 'safe'. We lose the sense of awe, wonder and mystery which is part of our created being. The colour and vibrancy of life are lost to us and we live in a world of faded dreams: God becomes simply one object among many in a dull world and all of this occurs because we think of God as an interfering person who constantly threatens to spoil our joy.

What God Is

Ignatius proposes an opposite image to the above: that of the gracious lover. From experience he asserts that when we take the risk of letting God be God - and it is a total risk - the lights go on and life begins to flow. God indeed becomes surprising, but the surprises are good rather than frightening. When we let God work freely, rather than spend our energies trying to prevent him working, then we bump into him everywhere and each mysterious encounter evokes awe, wonder and joy.

Instead of restricting God, we find ourselves begging God to work in us and through us and all around us. Our dreams take on a new freshness because they become the dreams of God. God becomes the centre of an endlessly fascinating world, and the deepest desire of our hearts is to find God in everything rather than to limit him in any way.

Sharing God's Dream

God is Trinitarian: there are three mysterious but totally good and infinitely resourceful persons at the heart of our world. Because they love us unconditionally they watch over us and over our world with infinite care, and engage with us in every detail of our lives. In one way, they are far ahead of us as they plan and labour for our good. From another point of view, they walk and work with us, guiding, supporting, sharing our burdens and keeping us going. They have a project, to which they are totally committed; they share it with us and invite our total response: their dream is to bring all humankind home in the final community of love.

For Ignatius, then, God is dynamic, eternally active, always making the first moves, the 'Divine Majesty', the Lord of all history and of all creation, and each of us is invited to help out in the completion of what God has in mind. Further, God is endlessly provident and supplies us, as trusted co-workers, with everything we need for the tasks given us. We have only to ask!

God Meets Us Face To Face

While God certainly blesses us richly with all we need for our tasks, Christian living is not to be reduced to simply working for God. The service or work must flow from *awareness of being loved by God and being in love in return.* God is 'the lover who shares with the beloved what he possesses', the Lord who 'desires to give himself to me.' For Ignatius, personal relationship with God is central and life becomes an invitation into limitless levels of intimacy and friendship with him. The quality of this loving relationship is not dependent on the quality of our service!

Here Ignatius might pause and tell you that the simplest and best way to get to know what God is really like is to speak with Jesus 'exactly as one friend speaks to another'

And so to the exercise that follows.

SUGGESTED EXERCISE

If you have followed the earlier exercises in this book, you will be growing in ease whenever you talk with Jesus.

● Again, imagine sitting with him, or walking together companionably and asking him about his Father. Your question, 'What is he really like?' might evoke the reply, 'You probably think that my Father is very different from me'. At this stage you might say, 'Yes, I feel comfortable with you, and I love what I have learnt about your openness, your willingness to take risks, your desire to bring me life, your friendship. Basically, I suppose I have come to know that you really do see me as your friend, that you understand me and my life; but would your Father also understand?' His smiling reply would surely be, 'But this is just the point! This is what my Father is like, I am just revealing him. "Like father like son" is absolutely true in our case'!

● 'Do you remember at my baptism, my Father said that I was his beloved son and he was very pleased with me? He could say this because I am the one who perfectly reveals what the Father is really like'.

● Ask Jesus for the grace to bring you into the mystery that knowing him is knowing the Father also (Jn 14:7).

Chapter Four

Where Love Is, There Is God

We are made for relationships! At the heart of our religion is God's loving relationship with us and our response to him. Some schools of spirituality focus more on certain religious practices and rules rather than on the personal experience which underlies and gives meaning to the relationship between God and ourselves. That God is to be found in particular practices is absolutely certain: the Mass, Communion, the sacrament of Reconciliation, devotion to the Sacred Heart, and the Rosary. All such practices can promote the vitality of our faith.

Strengths and Weaknesses

Surveys, however, reveal that in Ireland we are strong on the institutional level of faith, but weak on the mystical level. This means that many Irish Catholics have little sense that God is in love with them and they with God. It seems that personal experience of our relationship with God needs to be emphasised, and here Ignatian spirituality can help, because it stresses that we can experience our one-to-one relationship with God, and that we can also find God in all our experiences of life. Among our experiences are our religious practices: they are at their best when they flow from and express our relationship with

God. When you are in love you find all sorts of ways of showing it: some ways will be structured and others will be spontaneous. The important thing is that they should be alive rather than burdensome. God doesn't mind if you fall asleep while saying your prayers!

Experiencing Relationship

A woman said to me recently, 'All my life I have been involved in doing deals with God. If I said a certain number of prayers or performed tasks in set ways, then God would give me what I had earned. I have spent a long time explaining my life to God'!

When I asked her what she meant, she said, 'I thought it had to be all hard work and serious faces, a grinding slog. Now I have come to see Jesus standing in front of me, perhaps smiling a little wryly, waiting for me to stop working so hard at prayer, willing me to pause for breath, to lift my head and look at him, just to give him a chance to speak.'

'He lets me know that he understands about feelings, the loving and laughing, the loss and sadness. Events don't have to be sanitised before sharing the pain or the smile with him; the eyes don't have to be dried and the smile 'fixed' on! He might indeed shed a tear with me (and for me) if I could allow it. And I have also learned that he doesn't blush as easily as I thought he might, which is comforting'!

Centre of Her Life

This woman is catching on to her personal experience of God, and she is finding the relationship between herself and Jesus warm and real. If she lets it unfold, she will find this direct and intimate relationship with God becoming more and more the centre of her life. It is wonderful to her that an ordinary person like herself can be known and loved directly by God and that she knows and loves him directly too.

But she told me she fears that if she lets the relationship develop, she herself will be changed and she may lose contact with the other people in her life. She feels it is an 'either/or' situation: either God or the people in her life.

But the great richness of Ignatian spirituality is that it helps us both to cultivate our relationship with God and to recognise bit by bit that God is in all our other relationships. And not only is God in our human relationships, he is also in all our experiences of life. 'Finding God in all things and all things in God', is Ignatius' summary of these awesome truths. Let us unfold them a little.

Is God in Our Relationships?

God is most certainly in our relationships. The world of grace into which we are invited is a world of relationships, and so God's work with us centres on the developing of relationships. The three divine persons, who relate so perfectly with one another, want to extend their relating love to everyone. Therefore, when we are loved and love one another, we experience that relating love, and in this way we experience God as present in all our human relationships.

Quite simply, where love is, God is! In experiencing love in our lives, we are in fact experiencing God: when we experience that love is absent, we find in ourselves a yearning for it, and that yearning is a desire for God. 'To love another person is to see the face of God' - so goes the final song in *Les Miserables*. C. S. Lewis puts the same truth as follows: 'When we see the face of God we shall know that we have always known it. He has been a party to...all our earthly experiences of innocent love'.

God in Our Life Experiences

Can it be true that God is to be found everywhere? In holy places and in the kitchen? In school and in the waiting room of the health clinic? In examination halls and interview rooms? In the income tax office and in the dole queue? In parks and at the seaside? In police stations and courtrooms? In emergency rooms and maternity wards? In traffic jams and in supermarket check-outs and in the disco? In other words, can we find God in the day-to-day reality of our lives?

Some spiritualities doubt that God is present in our ordinary human experiences, but Ignatian spirituality holds that God is to be found, and wants to be found, in the flesh and blood of everyday life, just as he wanted to be found in the flesh and blood person named Jesus. Just as Jesus met his Father in the day-to-day experiences of his life, so also can we. This is why Ignatian spirituality is termed *incarnational,* which means en-fleshed. Each of us is an en-fleshed spirit, and we encapsulate a whole history and a wealth of experiences: within these we can search for God and be sure of finding him.

SUGGESTED EXERCISE

● Sometimes you have only a short space of time in your day for prayer: you could spend it in vocal prayer or in meditating on a passage of Scripture. This is good, but Ignatius, because he was so convinced that God is right beside us in the events of our day, suggests that you give the time over to reflecting on what is going on for you in your life right now. God is to be found in all your experiences, and if you stand back with him, he will help you to notice how he is present in them.

● So, settle down, perhaps in your friendly chair, and pull up another one for Jesus. Review the day with him, noticing with his help all the good that was in it, and since it is from him that all good things come, be grateful.

● But perhaps a bad event dominates your reflection: you had a row with someone you are close to and it ended badly. As you review the situation you realise that you were tired, and you know that when you are tired you are irritable. You also realise that you had been bottling up lots of anger rather than being more truthful earlier on; hence your explosion.

● You ask Jesus to teach you 'just as a schoolmaster teaches a child' (Ignatius' phrase about himself being taught by God) to find a way towards a more authentic relationship, even if it involves painful honesty. You decide to pray for the other person, and for yourself, and to watch that tiredness!

● Jesus rejoices that you have learnt something good from this unhappy experience, and you end by entrusting this difficult relationship to his healing grace.

Chapter Five

God In Everyday Things

Since God can be found in all things, he can be found in all the events and experiences of everyday life. But where, you may ask, does God choose to meet us? In the Church and the tabernacle, in the Sacraments and in devotions such as the Stations of the Cross and the Rosary? Certainly!

Everywhere A God-Zone

But God is to be found both when I am at Mass and when I miss Mass, when I am pious and when I am addled, when I am devout and when I am having a drink. The unemployed are no less valued by God than those who are blessed with work. Sexuality and family life are sacred no less than celibacy. Everywhere is a God-zone: all those bits of our lives which seem meaningless in themselves are being worked on by God so that they can have meaning within the vast story of human history.

Let us look in on an ordinary family, during a week full of things that just seemed to happen to them. We shall stay with Ann, the mother, as she looks back when it is all over and discovers, to her surprise, that she hadn't been alone. God was there!

On Sunday evening her son visited and his parents were glad to see him. He is twenty-two, has studied English at university but has now decided to work as a cleaner until he sells his first novel. He moved out last year. Casually, while sitting at the table he said he hoped to go back to university. His mother's heart missed a beat. She had always wanted him to get a proper job: could this be the answer? But he was penniless and wanted money for the application fee. With some misgivings - he smoked and drank any spare cash he had - they gave him the money.

Who Could It Be?

Each Monday Ann meets some friends to pray. On that particular night one of the group recounted the story of the abbot whose monastery had been famous for its holiness. But hard times had come and people no longer flocked there to nourish their spirit; the stream of young aspirants had dried up, the church was silent. Only a few sad and lonely monks remained.

When the abbot asked advice of a holy man, he was told that the situation had come about because of ignorance: one of the monks in the monastery was the Messiah in disguise and nobody recognised this fact.

Such excitement when he told his story to his companions! Imagine having the Messiah living with them. Who could it be? The holy man had said that the Messiah was in disguise, so each one's defects, clearly visible to all the others, had to be part of the disguise. Since they could not recognise him, they took to treating each other with great respect. After all, one never knew! The monastery was very soon filled with joy and love.

Ann loved the story and came home smiling. She was only in the door when her son rang to say he had lost his wallet that day: the money they had given him was in it.

And So It Goes

On Tuesday the ignition in the car let them down; on Wednesday the car had to be fixed and Ann's mother was taken ill, and so the week went on.

On Thursday a little boy who lives down the road stuck some wire into the lock on the boot of the car, so it was impossible to stow all the supermarket shopping.

Friday was like the other days: it rained all the time. The bus came too near the path and splashed dirty water over Ann's new coat. While all of these things were happening, the deeper problems of life remained to be dealt with; relationships still needed care, and someone close to Ann was going through a bout of bad depression. The hunger-filled eyes of refugee children stared out at her from the TV and the question floated around in her mind: 'Would the money, now lost, which we gave our son, have been better used if we had sent it off to help these starving children?'

When Saturday came, Ann got the lock on the car fixed. Later that morning they had two callers to the door asking for money; she gave what she could.

Not Another Knock!

In the early afternoon there was yet another knock. Looking out from an upstairs window she saw a very old man. Her heart sank: 'Not another sad story?' she thought. She whispered to her husband not to open the door. They waited. There was another knock. Her husband looked at her quizzically. 'But you always answer the door,' he whispered. Another knock, fainter now; the man was leaving. Husband and wife nodded to each other and he opened the door.

The old man turned and asked for their son by name. 'He doesn't live here now,' her husband said, 'but perhaps I can help.' 'I found his wallet on Monday last,' the old man said, 'and I waited until the weather improved to bring it to the address on his student card.'

He came in and sat down, and took a drink of fizzy orange. At eighty-four, he was in good health, and a great reader, though he had had little formal education. He thought that the loss of the library cards which he found in the wallet would be more important to the young man than the money. He held the young man's photo in his hands for quite a while and remarked: 'He'll be OK.'

God Has Been Busy

When the old man left, Ann and her husband were silent for a while: both had a sense that something mysterious was going on. They went out for a walk together and talked over what had happened. Ann had lived out her week in blind faith: it was one of many similar weeks and she had felt puzzled at times by the lack of joy in her world. She knew she was trying to find God, but sometimes, and for long periods, God seemed to be hiding - or even lost!

Now the old man's kindness was bringing a first glimmer of light and hope. She began to make connections: if their son had not been as he was he would not have needed the money, therefore he would not have lost it, and so the old man would never have come into their lives. Now the wallet was back; their son was affirmed by the old man, and husband and wife were drawn closer by all that had happened.

Even the old man had been helped: he had gone out of his way to respond when God had nudged him but he had enjoyed meeting the family, because he was a lonely man. Ann felt a sense of mystery pervading the events of the week and she is now finding it easier to say, 'God is busy behind the scenes!' Other events of that particular week still don't make any sense, but there are times when she can say, 'I often don't know why things happen, but it's all right'.

Her hope can survive chaos because she is catching on to the fact that God really does understand us and can bring good out of the messiness of our lives. She is almost daringly at ease with him, addressing him now as 'God of the chaotic and the unfinished!' She also knows that the Messiah called to their house that Saturday!

SUGGESTED EXERCISE

● Once again, find that place in which you can be quiet and where you are not likely to be disturbed for a while; sit or walk, and talk with Jesus.

● Tell him about your past week. Share with him how the days and nights unfolded, whether they were wonderful or not so good.

● The sharing of your memories and reflections with a friend, who has all the time in the world to listen to you, will be good.

● Ask Jesus to help you to see where he was in the living and loving, the discussing and arguing, the laughing and crying, the rushing and working, or, perhaps, in the enforced sitting or lying still.

● Speak as you would to someone who knows you and loves you, just as you are. The more regularly you do this, the more you will be convinced how absolutely dependable Jesus is. He is there for you, as he promised.

Chapter Six

How To Make Good Decisions

Let's take a pause at this stage of our pilgrimage to see where we are. We began with Ignatius coming to understand that he was very important to God: we noted that each of us is likewise important; that people make a difference, especially when they know that God is with them. When they gain confidence and freedom and a right sense of self-worth they move from passivity to wondering what God's dream for them might be. We then sketched out some images of God: the key to Ignatian spirituality is to catch on to the fact that God is dynamic and creative and ceaselessly active in our world. The three Divine Persons are always surprising us, especially by inviting us to be co-workers in the carrying through of their project - the ultimate happiness of humankind. We noted, however, that God invites us to personal intimacy as well as to task and service. Since the goal of Ignatian spirituality is 'to find God in all things', we outlined how God is to be found by reflection not only in 'religious' events but in all our everyday experiences and especially in our relationships.

What is emerging is that Ignatian spirituality is a journeying one. Ignatius was a journey-man, a traveller, a pilgrim. Not only did he walk the roads of Europe but he struggled along the paths of the inner journey in which a person encounters God. As you, the reader, allow yourself to be caught by this kind of spirituality, you find your own personal journey is under way.

Because your trust in God and your sense of being important to God are both growing, you are more willing to take risks. The willingness to take risks involves a sense of your own freedom, and a desire to use it for whatever seems best: you find yourself wanting to follow the prompting and beckoning of a companioning God, rather than staying 'at home' with what is safe and predictable simply because it is so.

Personal Choice

Choices follow, each of which brings you further along on your own inner journey. The journey is not mapped out beforehand: in fact there is no map and no road until you make your choices and set out.

The choices of others whose lives interact with yours affect your choices. You are not on a solitary pilgrimage: everyone else's choices affect you and your choices affect them. Yet each single choice is personal and often terrifyingly lonely: we would rather not have to bring pain into the lives of others and so we often postpone choices we know we should make. Yet we experience an inner obligation to take responsibility for our own truth and freedom.

Key to The Process

New levels of trust in God are demanded when not only your own life but the lives of those close to you are deeply affected by a decision that you make. Firstly, you are asked to believe that God will be able to bring good to the others through your decision. The image of an orchestra is inadequate but it can help here: all the musicians play the music written for them: it is the genius of the composer that-makes a symphony of what each person plays. But our 'music' is not written out for us beforehand: our lives become 'music' when we make decisions in accordance with conscience, and God orchestrates the 'music' of each of us into infinite harmony.

But how do we know when our choice is God's desire? This is where another level of trust is asked of us: that God is pleased with decisions arrived at in good conscience after prolonged and honest searching and prayer.

The key to the whole process is to believe that God desires only what is best for each and all of us; that God wants each and all of us to be happy and become our true selves. This is a massive act of faith in God's good will towards us: but if we make that act of faith, then we will want to help God to achieve this desire: why would we not want to make all our choices in line with what would be truly joyous for us?

Jesus Making Choices

Why did Jesus leave Nazareth to begin a new life as an itinerant preacher? Since he was human like ourselves, his searching for what would be pleasing to God must have involved him in reflection and prayer about what to do. We are told that he frequently took time out of busy days to be alone in prayer.

During the years in Nazareth he must have become steadily more aware of the depth of peoples' need for the Good News; did he then choose in freedom to risk sharing what he knew in the depth of his heart about God, namely that God is in love with humankind? In taking this step, he would be assuming responsibility for a new shape to his life and this choice would, he knew, radically affect his mother's life and that of the others around him. It was a hard choice, but did he experience it as emerging from an insistent need to be authentic? Not to follow it would have been to deny what was best in him.

Variety of Options

Sometimes Jesus was faced with a wide variety of options, as when he chose twelve apostles out of all the possible candidates. In the temptations in the desert, we see him freely choosing how he was going to live out his public life. In the agony in the garden we see him facing into a free but terrible choice. When we contemplate him on the cross, we can ask whether his freedom has now been totally taken from him: but we come to see that even when completely trapped and nailed down, he is choosing to accept patiently and lovingly a situation which he cannot change.

Attitude

When we find ourselves in situations over which we have no control and from which we cannot escape, we still have the freedom to choose how best to endure them, that is, in patient and loving trust. Suffering that cannot be avoided can still be redeemed. On Calvary one of the two criminals crucified with Jesus was screaming at him to save himself and them: the second criminal rebuked him: he could admit that his sufferings were a just punishment for his crimes and he could also turn to Jesus whom he believed to be innocent and ask his help. His suffering, though deserved in some way, was redemptive: it was bringing about a conversion of heart in him. Jesus, the innocent one, was enduring the same torture as the other two: his attitude was one of patient acceptance, of forgiveness and love. He could only hope that this attitude would be pleasing to his Father, and it was. It brought about the radical redemption of humankind.

We know this from the Resurrection: in raising Christ from the dead, the Father has gone guarantor that his son's free decision to accept patiently what was being done to him is the divinely chosen way to break the vicious circle of evil. The Resurrection is the enduring proof that love is the only right response to hate, that patience and kindness will soften human hearts, and that the golden rule of treating others as we would wish them to treat us is the only way to bring about the reconciliation of human beings with one another and with their God.

For Me?

We can perhaps accept that Jesus died for humankind: we can accept that Jesus would die for someone whom he loved intimately in his lifetime - Mary, for example, or Peter, or at least John. But for me? St. Paul believed that Jesus had died for him: 'He loved me and gave himself up for me' (Galatians 2:20). It has been well said that when we believe in the pronouns in that statement - 'he' and 'me' - our lives are transformed.

Freedom and Responsibility

The Spiritual Exercises are all about choices and how to make them well. Ignatius is trying to educate people to make decisions, both big and small, along the patterns of Jesus' decision-making. Ignatius believes that each individual decision is important because it affects the world. He is prepared, therefore, to spend much time helping people to understand that the gift of freedom with which God has endowed them can be put at the service of God's dream for them and for others.

He requires that retreatants face into the waywardness and disorder of their own freedom, but he encourages them to believe that a purified freedom is the best gift which we can offer to God in confident trust so that the two freedoms, God's and ours, can work harmoniously together. The image of two lovers, each responding to and evoking the best in the other, catches the point.

Ignatius invites retreatants to contemplate the life of Jesus, so that they can make decisions from within the same perspective as he did. Just as Jesus tried to please the Father in all his choices, so Ignatius proposes that 'the love which moves me and brings me to choose the matter in question should descend from above, from the love of God.

SUGGESTED EXERCISE

● When you are next alone with Jesus perhaps you might ask him how he felt when he knew he had to make the decision about leaving Nazareth. He was going to be different; his future was uncertain; his only certainty was his trust in God's love for him and for those whom he would meet.

● 'How was it for you, Jesus? Were you lonely, uncertain, afraid? You knew you would be different. Did you perhaps not like that feeling? Did you think that others would be uncomfortable with your being different?

● 'How did you come to terms with the heartbreak of leaving your mother whom you loved so dearly? Having made your choice, how much were you able to share with her about your dream? You must have known that her life and her relationships would be affected by your choice.'

● You might chat on these lines with Jesus, and perhaps also speak with Mary, asking her how she came to terms with her son's decision. Perhaps the three of you might chat together.

Chapter Seven

Hope For The World

Ignatian spirituality centres around the relationship between God, ourselves and our world. We have emphasised how important each person is to God, and how God has chosen to need us and to make use of all we are and all we can offer in shaping the story of humankind.

We have noted that God as revealed in Scripture and in Ignatius' own experience is dynamic and actively involved in every detail of the world: God 'labours' for us in all things and invites us to labour with him.

By looking in on the life of an ordinary family we have noticed that God is not distant and remote but present in our experience, in the everyday details of human living and relationships.

We have unfolded a little more the basic Ignatian theme of *finding God in all things* by asking how we can make well-informed choices which will bring us into harmony with what God wants for the world.

A Good or Bad World?

Our theme in this chapter is how Ignatian spirituality views the world.

As I write, a newspaper headline hits me: 'God is sleeping in the nightmare that is Rwanda.' The murder of up to one million people in a savage civil war raises huge issues, with which any authentic spirituality today must grapple. Is the world good, bad or indifferent? What is God's attitude to the world? Or, as a child put it recently, 'What does God do all day?'

The world reacts with horror to situations such as Rwanda, and believing people ask: 'Why does God allow this sort of thing to happen?' But deeper reflection brings out the fact that every one of those killings was a free choice. This makes us wonder whether God should have given us the gift of freedom at all? But a world of programmed automatons would be emptied of what we hold most dear: freedom, love, trust, respect, commitment. So now the issue is: how is human freedom to be rightly developed so that our choices promote the good of humankind?

Realistic and Hopeful

Ignatian spirituality offers a perspective on the world that is both realistic and hopeful: it is the divine view, and if we can catch on to it we will find it possible to make wise choices.

Doesn't it surprise us that the Three Divine Persons can be realistic and hopeful about our world? For we can often feel like despairing of our world because its brokenness and messiness are pounding us endlessly, and we feel powerless to change things for the better.

But when we catch on to the idea that God both knows the misery of the human situation and still has hope for the world then hope is rekindled in us.

Why does God still hope? Because he is totally committed to our world, and makes decisive choices which transform it. Although we feel helpless in the face of the anti-human forces which dominate our world, God empowers us to make choices which are often very difficult and demanding and so we become his collaborators in bringing the world to rights.

A Flawed Masterpiece

The world is undeniably flawed and disordered, but it is a flawed masterpiece which God will always love: it is our world and it is humankind in all its concreteness that God intends to transform.

'God loved the world so much that he gave his only Son, so that everyone who believes in him may not be lost but may have eternal life' (Jn 3:16).

There are two wonderful pieces of good news in this short statement. The first tells us what God is like - he is the person who loves the people of this world so much that he gives over his only Son for our sakes. The Son, of course, is not a passive victim as the child Isaac was in the Genesis story: rather, we should think of the Son as totally agreeing with the Father's desire to save the world, and as giving himself over freely and lovingly for our sakes.

The second piece of good news is a revelation of the destiny to which every inhabitant of our tiny planet is called - we are made for the enjoyment of divine company and boundless happiness together. The Three Divine Persons invest themselves totally in the achievement of this project. They work at it all the time. Determined to succeed in it, they are undaunted by the difficulties and resistances which we can place in their way.

The process of our restoration and that of the whole material world is irrevocably under way, and all people of good will are invited to participate in this enterprise. Jesus is revealed to his contemporaries as the one who is totally given over to the fulfilment of the enterprise of God and we in turn as his disciples are meant to be likewise available to God and eager to do his will for the good of the world.

Getting Involved

Ignatian spirituality is incarnational: this means that just as the presence of God was enfleshed 2,000 years ago in the person of Jesus, so our spirituality must become enfleshed today. (Incarnation means, 'in the flesh'). Incarnational spirituality means a willingness and desire to be engaged with humankind in all its struggles, whereas a 'disincarnate' spirituality would remain safe, distant and unengaged.

Ignatius invites us to focus continually on the person of Jesus and to follow his way: he is the one who becomes fully human, who lives, walks and talks with companions, prays, feels love and friendship, becomes angry, cries, puzzles over choices, and, like each one of us, is affected by other peoples' choices. Human relationships mean everything to him and he is constantly encouraging people to become more loving with one another and with God.

Facing Conflict

Jesus' world, like our own, was full of conflict. How did he conduct himself in it? He comes across as someone who has hope for everyone: he sees and affirms the hidden potential in the worst of people, the 'sinners' who come flocking to him. Because he believes in people, they come to believe in themselves.

He is not against anyone, but he challenges people to become aware of what is false in themselves, so that they may become free of it. He works for the radical cure of the human heart rather than glossing over our inner sickness with rituals and pious practices. He labours to purify and liberate the human spirit and to entice it to desire the fullness of life, the life of glory and of happiness which his Father wants for us all.

When people reject and persecute him he doesn't become embittered and hardened against them: instead he chooses to reveal a totally unmerited reserve of forgiving love which may eventually melt the most stubborn hearts. In this patient enduring of what is done to him the fullness of love is revealed: two loves coincide, divine love and human love. And this love is limitless; it bursts all boundaries, and it is all for the world.

Homeward Course

Secular history is caught up into sacred history by the incarnation of God in Jesus. Not only does God wish the world well, but the Son has radically redeemed it and set it on its homeward course. There is nothing profane about it; none of it is irrelevant to God. Therefore we can find God everywhere in the world. True, the world is full of famines and disasters, murders, violence and terrorism, but it is also full of surprises and goodness. Awe, wonder, reverence and excitement should characterise all our dealings with it because the deep down mystery of the world is that it is infinitely loved.

SUGGESTED EXERCISE

● By now you will be used to spending some particular time sitting or walking, and talking with Jesus.

● Recalling what you have just read, and speaking exactly as one friend speaks to another, you might ask Jesus how it felt to walk the journey to Calvary.

● 'Apart from the physical pain, how were you feeling? What were you thinking?'

● 'Were there times on the journey when you couldn't believe that your life would end here?'

● 'Death on a cross: why? You had spoken of love and the possibility of good relationships between all people: how could it all go so sour?'

● 'Was it a terrible struggle for you to choose not to be bitter or hard or condemnatory?'

● `Dear Jesus, I am struggling like you with the pain of broken dreams. Help me to have the right attitude in this situation, which I cannot avoid.

You must have hated what you had to go through, yet you endured it patiently and with forgiving love. Give me the grace to live and act like you.'

Chapter Eight

Companions Of Jesus

Our topic in this chapter is Jesus, because he is the centre of Ignatian spirituality. He is the person who, more than anyone else in human history, gets involved with God and with the world.

He accepts fully his own value as given to him by his Father, who says to him, 'You are my dearly loved son'. In other words, 'You are important!' Jesus knows in a unique way what God is like.

Wonderful Truth

He labours to reveal to a stubborn and resisting people the wonderful truth about God and God's concerns for the world. Jesus experiences human life to the full: he learned from his mother to reflect on experience and to search for God even in what seemed meaningless and disgraceful. Thus, in chatting with the two disciples on the road to Emmaus he interprets his Passion in a meaningful and graced way. Throughout his life we see him struggling to make wise choices no matter how demanding they may be.

The incident of the temptations in the desert summarises his lifelong effort to keep in tune with his Father's desires for him, and he can truly say, 'I always do what pleases him'. He is realistic and hopeful about the world and believes so much in people that he is willing to die so that they may be freed to achieve the wonderful destiny that the Father wishes for them.

A Personal Relationship

In learning about Ignatian spirituality, then, we are really trying to catch on to the mystery of Jesus himself. Ignatius keeps pointing to Jesus, never to himself. He is much more interested in facilitating our relationship with Jesus than in constructing an abstract theory of spirituality.

It has been said that his genius lies in his capacity to attract people who have strong desires and a high level of imagination - people who can see things in colour rather than in black and white, and in three dimensions rather than in two.

Through the *Spiritual Exercises* he uses all kinds of helpful ways to enable such people to focus on the Jesus of the Gospels. The process initiates a transformation: retreatants find themselves won over to Jesus, not only on the level of intellect and will, but on the levels of imagination, affectivity, feelings and emotions. Quite simply, a falling in love goes on: deep engagement leads to intimate appreciation of Jesus, so that his vision and values and attitudes are assimilated.

Ignatius, in other words, has a special gift to help people to identify with the mind and heart of Jesus, so that for the rest of their lives they will want their choices to coincide with the desires of God. He believes that if we watch carefully and lovingly the life of God-become-human we will know how to live: Ignatian spirituality fosters Christian discipleship, and that is why it is found to be so helpful to an incredible variety of people, in fact to anyone trying to live out a Christian life.

Companions of Jesus

It becomes clear from the above why Ignatius insisted that the name of his little group must be *'Companions of Jesus'* rather than *'Ignatians'*. His guiding image was that of Jesus and his apostolic band, who were to be with him and also sent out. 'Companions of Jesus' is a description not, of course, reserved to Jesuits but open to all who identify with the values of Jesus and who gather together to support one another and to work out by discernment what Jesus may want them to do.

The word 'companions' literally means a group, whether small or large, formal or informal, who break bread together. The first Jesuits saw themselves as 'friends in the Lord': for each of them their relationship with Jesus was primary, and this love made it easy for them to love one another, and it inspired everything they did. Like them, we can 'break bread' with Jesus and with one another, and deliberate in his presence how we can best bring his love to a needy world.

Into Our World

The goal of Ignatian spirituality, as we have said before, is to find God in all things. Before the Incarnation people might well have been justified in thinking that God could be found only beyond this world: as the 'Holy One'. God was considered distant, inaccessible, and almost, as it were, keeping the divine hands clean from the messiness of human situations.

But with the Incarnation the place where God wishes to be found is here! We don't have to look up to heaven to find God, but to look around us: distance has disappeared, and God is immediately present, as close to us as our neighbours. The treasure, the pearl of great price, is not hidden in some distant place but in ourselves and in the person next to us. Everything about our lives is God-touched and important. The human and divine are meant to be as inseparable in us as they are in Jesus.

Our task in the world is to help others to catch on to all the implications of this mystery. The struggle for human dignity becomes our central concern, as it was for Jesus, but the fullness of that human dignity is found only when the divine dimension of our lives is fully realised. The task of Christians is to be carriers of this mystery of human value.

The Right Place To Be

That God has come in person among us transforms our world and gives it hope. Things can never be the same again: a light shines in the darkness, and the darkness cannot smother it; instead, it will transfigure the darkness and all will become light. The world is now the right place to be in, if we want to meet God.

Since God has become human, we can encounter him in everything that is human - all points of interaction between human beings have now become privileged meeting places with God. Every place, no matter how unlikely, where we find human beings, is a holy place: hospitals for instance, where people are born and healed and suffer and also die; waiting places, whether nursing homes, prisons, refugee camps, bus stops, dole queues or queues for confession; tables for meals and meetings, and human celebrations.

Furthermore, God is involved in all relationships, not as a polite observer but creatively and warmly: whatever is good and constructive in the relationship is the work of God's grace. We find him in the friendship of marriage, in its loyalty, fidelity and durability which are most evident in times of stress. And insofar as genuine friendship exists in any relationship, even though it may not conform to established norms, God is involved.

A Dangerous Prayer

You probably know the prayer commonly attributed to Ignatius, which begins:

'Dear Lord, teach me to be generous,
To give and not to count the cost.'

There is in fact no evidence that Ignatius composed this prayer, and, taken out of the context which we have outlined above, it can be very harmful.

Quite simply, Ignatian spirituality flows from a falling in love with the Son of God because he has first loved me. Without this awareness of a loving relationship, Ignatian spirituality would become a heartless and grinding service in which all is being asked of me. Why should I 'do the holy will' of God in the demanding ways suggested by this prayer?

God Always Leads

The only adequate reason would be that I have become aware that God, as an extravagantly generous lover, gives everything to me, the beloved: overwhelmed with gratitude, I want to respond out of love. But the manner of my responding will not be dictated by some heroic decisions of my own making, but rather by a sensitive 'Yes' to what God invites and enables me to do.

For Ignatius, God always leads: the goal is not to strike out on our own but to follow Jesus: he will always give us the 'love and grace' required to respond rightly to what he asks.

SUGGESTED EXERCISE

● See Jesus at a distance coming towards you. He holds out his hand as you approach each other. Perhaps he is a little breathless as he moves to greet you: he is eager and smiling and you feel that he is happy to meet you.

● Feel the warmth and strength of his hand clasped in your own.

● As you walk or sit with him, can you allow yourself to take a risk? There is a risk in telling a friend how you feel about him or her.

● The phrase 'I simply love you' hangs in the air. Can you say it? Can you hear Jesus say it to you?

● Spend some time in letting this tentative encounter develop.

Chapter Nine

How To Listen To God

A recent biographer of Ignatius has emphasised that he had the ability 'to listen attentively and carefully to an inner Presence deep within his being...He was a perpetual, sensitive listener to the word of God, to an internal word strengthened by joy and peace'.

Inner Presence

Can we become like that? Is it possible for us to learn from Ignatius how to become ever more sensitive to the 'inner Presence' deep within our beings? The answer is a very definite 'Yes'. Ignatius himself encourages us and offers us helpful guidelines on how to listen to what is going on inside us so that we can more easily find our way forward and make our choices well.

At first, we may catch on only occasionally to the fact that God is present for us, helping and guiding us. But with practice, we can remember more spontaneously and turn, almost without thinking, as Ignatius did, 'to listen attentively and carefully to an inner Presence deep within'.

Ignatius was not only in communication with God during prayer and when offering Mass, but he also grew steadily in his capacity to find God in all things. Shortly before he died in his mid-sixties, he acknowledged that whenever he wished, at whatever hour, he could find God. We, too, can become more comfortable with God as a cherished life-companion who shares every detail of our lives.

I Am Never Alone

I can come to a deep awareness that the Holy Spirit is for me, personally and uniquely; that he is aware of my particular situation and where I am right now. I don't have to be in the 'correct place' in order to meet with my Holy Spirit: I don't have to reach some level of holiness such as the saints did before being able to experience the intimate presence of the Spirit. No, the Holy Spirit is glad to be with me, in my present situation: he would not prefer to be with someone more interesting or important: he wants to be with me, to encourage me, to prompt me and to draw me to what is good.

'You have made us for yourself, and our hearts are restless until they rest in you.' So Augustine said, but we misunderstand him if we think he meant that our hearts will remain restless until we meet God at the end of our lives. In fact, our hearts can rest in God throughout our lives; at this very moment, even as you read these words, you can be resting in God and believe that God gazes on you and smiles. Try it!

Do you honestly believe that God smiles on you? That God is both realistic and hopeful about you, as we said in an earlier chapter? Isn't it easier to believe that God shakes his head in disappointment over the mess you always seem to be in? The reality is that God is sad for our very real pain, but never, never gives up on us: his hand is always outstretched, encouraging us gently to try again.

As we grow older, and become more aware, we can look back on life and see that there were times when we had it all wrong, even when we thought we were acting wisely and correctly. At such times it is so good to know that God is still present, and was present in the dark days.

Recognising His Presence

The following testimony is a good example of how we can grow in this sort of awareness.

'My daughter was ill for eight years when she was a child. My prayer was constant and desperate: 'Make my little girl better - Now!' I believed that God would be there for my daughter, but I had no sense at the time that he was there for me. I couldn't catch on to the way in which he was trying to guide me, even through her illness. He was offering me something good but I was fixated on one thing - an immediate miracle.

Only slowly did I catch on to certain values which I would have missed if I had not been in that situation. For instance, illness was considered shameful in our family, but through meeting other people with similar problems I came to accept that illness is part of life. In the waiting rooms and clinics, as parents shared their troubles, supported each other through difficult times and rejoiced whenever the news was good, I learned the true value of people.

I now see that God was intensely present to me and involved, but I had no awareness that I could have leaned on him and asked him to put his arm around me while my daughter was enduring those terrible tests. But now he and I sit together in waiting rooms and at the end of beds: mothers wait a lot, but they need not wait alone.'

'You were with me but I was not with you.' This was Augustine's conclusion as he reflected over his sinful years: God was with him even then, in his sinning, but he had distanced himself from God.

Another Name For God

If someone asked you to give them another word for 'God', you could use the word 'Presence', for that is what God is. When Moses asked Yahweh his name, Yahweh replied, 'I am who am' and this means 'I am present'. God is really saying, 'I shall be there for you'. God is intimately present to everything, and especially to us. God's name is Emmanuel, which means 'God is with us'. Matthew's Gospel ends with the marvellous statement: 'Know that I am with you always; yes, to the end of time'.

Consolation

If God is totally present to us, can we in turn be present to God, aware of God, focused on God? Surely yes: God is a self-revealing God, who wants us to know he is there for us, and wants us to catch on to his presence. Ignatian spirituality helps us to become aware of God's presence: the more this awareness grows, the easier it is for us to 'find God in all things'. When you are aware of how God makes his presence felt you become alert to looking out for these signs.

Ignatius uses the term consolation to indicate the way we are when we are tuned into God. Consolation can be described in many ways: a sense of harmony, peace, appropriateness: 'I'm together'. Energy is focused on what is good and loving: strength and courage are present and a feeling of being able to cope, even though a decision may bring difficulty. 'I'm facing the right way now.' There is a sense of being in the light rather than in the dark about the way forward. Such are some of the indicators of God's presence, and we can become aware of them.

Desolation

The contrary to consolation is desolation. It is as if the light had gone out and you are left in the dark. You sense that God is absent. You are out of sorts, off-key or off-centre, you are in a spin, fragmented and moody, preoccupied with inner struggles, missing out on joy, seeing things as grey or black; you feel unsure, unhappy, separated and lonely; it is hard to be loving and kind, and easy to put bad

interpretations on everything. You lose courage and your
judgements can be quite unbalanced and negative. Clearly,
in desolation your demons are hard at work, whereas in
consolation your good spirit is leading.

Notice that it is easier to describe desolation than consolation! When we are in our dark moods, we think we are
darkness: we identify ourselves with it. 'I am bad, useless,
out of place.' It would help so much if we could distinguish ourselves from the mood: the next time you feel des-
olate, try the following, 'I have a bad mood; I, who am
good, have a bad mood. But it will pass, and I will come
back to my true self soon. I am in the dark now, but the
light will soon shine again.'

Walking in the Light

The point is that God wants us to be in consolation, not
in desolation nor in some grey area in between. We are
made for God and when we are faced towards God we are
in consolation - we are in the light, in tune with God, on
track, in the right place, no matter where we happen to be
physically.

Consolation is not essentially about feeling nice and
comfortable, though such feelings can accompany it.
Rather it is basically about being with God. It can be present as much in the wintry times of our lives as in the
bright times: the wind which blows my boat to its harbour
can be cold and piercing or a gentle breeze: either will do -
what matters is that I am on course, and moving towards
God. Peace and harmony can often be deep down and you
need then to search for them beneath the turbulence on the
surface.

At the end of his prayer in the Garden, Jesus was at
peace at the deepest level of his being: he was in consolation, even though he must have been very distressed on the
levels of emotion and feeling.

A Sense of Peace

Try to identify moments that bring a smile or a sense of peace: you will interpret them rightly as moments of consolation. Be aware of them as 'God-moments', for they carry the touch of God, the smile of God, the nod of God's gratitude or approval.

SUGGESTED EXERCISE

● As you go about your day, chat it along with Jesus. As events occur, share them with him:

● 'Jesus, I'm going to go for this interview...'

● 'I'm lying here alone and in pain...'

● 'I'm looking forward to the big match...'

● 'I'm going to feed the baby...'

● 'Jesus, I'm stuck. I don't know what to do...'

Doing this helps to bring Jesus into the day, moment by moment: he is there for me and I am there for him. It is a companionship.

● Pray for the grace to believe that it is so, because it surely is.

● You might also read about the calming of the storm in St Matthew's Gospel, Ch. 8: 23-27. The panic-stricken disciples felt they were going to drown: they were in desolation. In desperation they turned to Jesus, who was there all along, and he made everything calm again: they were restored to consolation.

Chapter Ten

Like A Falling Tear

Imagine a pilot of a plane or ship peering into the mist in order to see the way ahead; there you have a simple image of discernment. The pilot needs to see through the cloud to the underlying reality; to see deeply, in order to recognise and distinguish the various contours, and so to find the path safely. Another image, used in the early days of the Church, was of money-changers discerning good coins from counterfeit ones: they sifted through the heap of coins, with an accurate eye for the good and the bad.

What is Discernment?

The gift of discernment, then, is the capacity to distinguish the good from the bad, especially when the bad is dressed up under the appearance of good. Since Ignatian spirituality is centred on finding God through the making of good decisions, discernment is central to it. Different options can seem both good and attractive: how can we know which of them has God's approval?

Personal Experience

Ignatius offers guidelines to help us to discern our way forward, and these come from his reflection on personal inner experience. In the last chapter we looked at consolation and desolation, and you were invited to notice these inner states, these feelings and moods, in your own experience.

Did you notice times and situations and perhaps choices which carried with them a sense of energy, peace and joy? And was there not a movement forward in the way of true love? Perhaps you spent time with a sick person, even though you had many other things to do, or perhaps you were feeling sorry for yourself, and, having wallowed in your misery for a while, you turned to God and begged for help, and found yourself stronger and freer as a result?

Sense of Direction

Since we are made for God, turning to God will always bring consolation, that is, strength, peace, courage, togetherness. For when we move towards God, we are 'on our thread', 'on the right wavelength'.

Homing pigeons, when released from their cages hundreds of miles from home, will circle for a while, and then unerringly find their true direction and follow it through thick and thin until they land, perhaps exhausted, where they belong. We are a bit like homing pigeons!

Just as something deep within assures the birds that they are on the right path, so in us the experience of consolation assures us that we are moving in God's direction, or more simply in the direction of love.

Spiritual Consolation

As an aside, it is important to note that by consolation Ignatius always means spiritual consolation, the consolation of the Good and Holy Spirit of God. There are other consolations: that of the addict getting another 'fix' or that of the bank-robber who gets away with a big haul. Their feelings of joy, satisfaction or peace are not from God: they are mere surface consolations, masking deep inner unhappiness and desolation.

This fact brings us to yet another insight about ourselves and how we can find our way more securely: the experience of desolation can be helpful insofar as it makes us realise that we are going the wrong way: it is saying, 'Wrong Way! Go Back!'. On motorways, such signs are frightening but helpful: they save lives.

Through Darkness to Light

An example of how desolation can befriend us. An authoritarian priest was asked by some parishioners to meet with them. The meeting was a heated one: the honest anger of the parishioners disconcerted the priest, who went off feeling shattered and depressed.

Days passed. At times he felt like punishing the people and asserting himself as 'The Boss'. At other times their final words at the meeting played on his heart: 'We love you, Father, and we respect you for all you do for us. But we want our needs to be taken into account'. 'We love you', they said, and they showed it by their gentle sensitivity, while he struggled in his valley of darkness.

Finally he yielded to the Good Spirit, and in a homily which was at once both painful and joyous, he told what had happened and proposed a meeting - which would be chaired by a laywoman! - to share on how to work together as a parish.

Thus desolation can be a pathway to true consolation. Never ignore desolation: it is trying to tell you something you need to know, just as physical pain does.

His Eyes Were Opened

Ignatius discovered this while convalescing at Loyola in 1521: he whiled away many hours thinking of his lady-love and what he might do to impress her, but though these dreams gave him much delight, he would find, when he put them aside, that he was dry and dissatisfied. But when he thought of imitating the austerities of the saints and of walking barefoot to Jerusalem, not only was he consoled while he had these thoughts, but even after putting them aside he remained 'satisfied and joyful.' Desolation versus Consolation!

But much time passed, he tells us, until 'his eyes were opened a little and he began to marvel at the difference and to reflect upon it, realising from experience that some thoughts left him sad and others joyful. Little by little he came to recognise the difference between the spirits that were stirring, one from the evil spirit, the other from God'.

Discerning Hearts

I suggest that we all have such experiences: contrary influences 'stir' us, and it is a great help to us if we reflect on them and see where each is leading. Thus we become persons of discerning hearts, which is what Paul asked for the Philippians: 'In my prayers I ask that your love may lead you each day to a deeper knowledge and clearer discernment, that you may have good criteria for everything. So you may be pure of heart and come blameless to the day of Christ' (Phil. 1:8-10). By 'heart' we mean the centre within us from which our convictions flow.

Drops of Water

In a delightful image, Ignatius contrasts the action of the good and bad spirits on a sincere heart. 'The good spirit touches the soul gently, lightly, sweetly, like a drop of water falling on a sponge. The evil spirit touches it sharply, with noise and disturbance, like a drop of water falling on a stone'. A drop of water, a tear, is a tiny thing: try noticing how it falls differently on absorbent or hard surfaces - lots of silent attention is demanded!

Similar attention is demanded to notice the action of the Good Spirit on our hearts, but the reward is that we can move along securely in the ways of God, and help others to do so too. God is constantly drawing us, tugging at our hearts, quietly beckoning, working silently in all things for our good, and we can find him through attending to our own hearts. Savour this wonderful mystery: your heart is a holy place where God and yourself can always meet!

The Great Conflict

Especially when things are hard, we need to know that a good influence is at work in us, countering the negative and destructive influences that are all too obvious. We can feel small and helpless in the great conflict between what is good and what is anti-human and anti-divine, but the Holy Spirit is steadily present to us, helping us, and others through us, to realise our high destiny, which is to be sons and daughters of God.

The Holy Spirit does not remove us from the conflict to a safe place. Rather the conflict is in us and around us, but the Spirit evokes the best in us and gives us, through consolation, the signs we need to stay close and act rightly with God, who labours to transform situations and structures which are de-humanising, ungraced and ungodly.

We Need Consolation

Ignatius spent the last phase of his life co-ordinating his newly-founded *Company of Jesus,* making important decisions which were to transform the lives of many people across the world. The early Jesuits saw themselves as engaged in a ministry of consolation: they had learnt for themselves what consolation was like - they experienced it as the energy, purpose and joy which came from being united with God in all they were trying to do, no matter how difficult the task or how daunting the opposition.

They must have echoed Ignatius' remark that 'he could not live without consolation' by which he meant, not euphoria and a feeling of being on top of the world, but an inner conviction that what he was about, even if humble, painful and laborious, was pleasing to God. Like Jesus, he asked no more and no less than this.

SUGGESTED EXERCISE

● This time, as you pray in your quiet place, imagine walking toward Jesus as he stands alone overlooking Jerusalem, Luke 19:41-44. Slowly, you become aware of the fact that he is weeping.

● How would you feel if you were to put your arm around his shoulder as he bows his head? Could you wipe his tears?

● You listen as he speaks about the hard-heartedness of the people that he loves so much. He is tempted to give up, to despair, to turn away and distance himself from them. He needs to call on new dimensions of love, the existence of which he is hardly aware of. Otherwise, he will slide into desolation.

● Can you be with him now? Can you say to him: 'I also know what it's like to have to dig deeper than I ever believed was possible to find enough love and courage to keep going.' How does Jesus respond to you?

Chapter Eleven

Living Prayer

Jesus asks us to pray at all times (Lk 21:36). This can seem an impossible task, because we have so much 'living' to do, but Ignatian spirituality helps to make it more manageable, because it guides us into seeing that real Christian living is an open communication with God in everything that goes on. It sees no dualism between prayer and life: it cultivates the attitude of an undivided heart that looks towards God in everything. God wants to be with us; He is always coming into our lives as they evolve; He wants us to search and seek for him in every situation, to involve him. Real life for us lies here because human life is all about relationships and most deeply about our relationship with God. So to discover God even in an everyday detail is a life-giving experience for us; it is a prayer.

God Is Involved

But have you this sense right now that God is involved in your life?

You may feel only half-alive, weak and sad, lost and alone, burdened and frightened. It can seem impossible to make a prayer within this miserable situation. God seems so distant that it would be impossible to reach Him: you haven't got the energy to search for Him. But can you allow yourself to believe the amazing truth that God is passionately searching for you at this moment in the depths of the mess and despair? God knocks on your locked door, asking to be admitted into your life, offering to share your burden and to companion you through the darkness. Can you allow God to love you, to respect you, to give you back your integrity and your hope? Can you accept the dignity of being a friend of God and believe that this is one friendship which need never fail?

Did Jesus feel something like this in his Passion? How did he manage to keep going when everything seemed lost? He was helped by the fact that his whole life up to this point was a living prayer. This was because in everything he did and in all that happened to him he was looking out for his Father: they loved each other. He wanted so much to please his Father. The Father was the centre of his life and this gave a fresh and wonderful meaning to everyone and everything in his world. Because he involved him in all he did, everything in his life, both the joyous and the painful, was a living prayer. So when everything fell apart around him in the Passion, the centre still held: Father and Son were still together, still totally for one another.

Love Is The Reason

For Ignatius, everything done with a pure intention of serving God, is a living prayer. So a task we undertake in the sincere belief that this is what God wants, is not less pleasing than private prayer, and may even be more so. Seeking and finding God in all things is the primary issue for us, just as it was for Jesus: it leads to a life which is transparently open to God and available for whatever God wants. God and God's desires are put first, and the reason is love. In this way, we become a living prayer. The grace which surrounds and enfolds our lives, and which enables us to become fully what we are intended to be, the sons and daughters of God, comes to have fuller and more unrestricted play in our lives.

Private Time With God

Now that we are clear about the ways in which our whole life can become a living prayer, we can consider those private times with God which are essential. We need time alone with a person in order to develop a relationship with them. For a friendship to deepen, the two persons need time alone with each other; time to talk and time to listen; time to explore each other's lives and to catch on to their different values, attitudes and preferences. Self-disclosure is of the essence of friendship; each becomes vulnerable. 'Will I be accepted just as I am? The truth of me is not all I would wish it to be. Will I be *handled with care?* Will my dignity survive the gaze of the other?'

As One Friend To Another

Ignatius had a deep capacity for friendship, and he brought this into his relationship with God. He suggests that we begin our prayer by noticing how God sees us, and for him God sees us as a lover sees a dearly beloved. God, the great lover, wishes for nothing but the good of the beloved and wants to share everything with us. Thus at the beginning of prayer, two friends gaze on one another: each is glad of this meeting, because it is a precious time. The whole prayer unfolds within this context of two friends meeting: self-disclosure follows. I tell God about myself and how I am and what my dreams and my difficulties are. As Ignatius says, I make known my affairs to God and seek advice in them. I ask God for what I want and desire, and especially that everything about me may be directed purely to His praise and service.

When I have come to an end of what I want to say, and God has listened reverently as a good friend will, I invite God to communicate with me.

How does God do this? Most obviously, God speaks to me through Scripture. I may choose the Mass reading of the day and ask God for light to see how it speaks to my situation; or if it is an event from Jesus' life, I may enter into it imaginatively and allow myself to be changed by meeting with Jesus in the scene. At another time, it may be that through inviting the Father or Jesus to listen to my experience, I come to see where he is hidden in it, since he is present in all my experiences. It may be, too, that I spend time asking for what I know I need: perhaps the gift of forgiveness, or courage or generosity or whatever. There are also companionable silences. It may seem that nothing is going on in this simple being-with, but heart is speaking to heart at a level too deep for words, and I am changed in the process.

God Leads in Prayer

Ignatius has often been accused of rigidity in setting out methods of prayer: his instructions for beginners are concise, but he never intended them to constrict further development. All he wanted to do was to help people to get directly in touch with God: he then stepped aside, for he believed that the only teacher of prayer is the Holy Spirit. 'God sees and knows what is best for each one...and shows each the road to take...so that a person goes forward by that way which for them is the clearest and happiest and most blessed in this life.'

Reflecting On the Day

People who are busy for God, and because God wants them to be busy, will sometimes not have much time for the kind of prayer described above. Ignatius advises such people to take even a little time out in the course of the day to reflect on what has been going on in the *busyness*. He called this exercise the *Examen*. It includes: a prayer to the Holy Spirit for light to catch on to the meaning of the day's experiences: gratitude for the blessings which God has given during the day: reflection on the ways in which

God has been leading in the various events: sorrow for the ways in which we have lost track of God; and finally, a looking forward to the following day in joy and trust that God will be with us at every moment of it.

SUGGESTED EXERCISE

● 'Good morning!'........'Hello again!'........'Good evening!'

Can prayer be simpler than this? Try it.

● 'Good morning!'

'I come to you to take your touch before I begin my day' (R. Tagore).

My actual situation may be no better than it was yesterday but it helps so much to know that God has been waiting for me to wake up to wish me a good morning and I'm happy to respond in my own words. God is a Good Morning God!

● 'Hello again!'

The centre doesn't change. God is always present and involved. I take a moment whenever I can to smile at God and acknowledge gratefully that He is near, ready to help if needed.

● 'Good evening!'

'God, here we are together again; it's been quite a day. Let's look over it and see it through one another's eyes. I tend to focus on the dark patches, so let me not lose sight of the good things. Turn on the light and show me how you have been leading me: remain patient with me because I am learning, slowly!

'Here's to tomorrow! See you in the morning.'

Chapter Twelve

With Love Beyond All Telling

This chapter was originally written for a December issue of the *Sacred Heart Messenger*. I have retained the Christmas flavour because we need to get in touch over and over again with the innocence, freshness, and rebirth that this season signifies.

The central message is that God is coming into our world because He loves us. The birth of Jesus is a gentle event in one way, but explosive in another: his coming turns everything inside out and upside down. Perhaps poets catch the point better than the rest of us: one of them, a Latin American, put it thus:

'I searched for God in the heavens,
  but I found He had fallen to earth.
So now I must search for Him among my friends.'

God is in our material world, God is in everything that is human, God's history and our history merge together through the incarnation of the son of God. Our understanding of God, our world and ourselves is transformed, and Ignatian spirituality is no more and no less than an effort to put words on this transformation.

All Things New

For Ignatius, everything was transformed in a basic way through an experience which God gave to him at Manresa in 1522, and the rest of his life was an unfolding of that radical experience. God revealed to him how He is present in all things: it was a mind-blowing experience which came out of the blue to a convalescent pilgrim as he was making his devotions. He wasn't ready for it and later found it hard to talk about, and yet years later when asked why he was deciding things in one way or another, he would reply, perhaps with a smile, 'The explanation will be found in something that happened to me at Manresa.' From his stumbling words we can gather the following: he was given a profound appreciation of the most Holy Trinity, and of the Incarnation of the Son and how he is present in the Eucharist. Next, 'the manner in which God created the world was revealed to his understanding with great spiritual joy'. Lastly, his mind was illuminated regarding 'spiritual things and matters of faith and of learning'. He notes that from this time on everything seemed new to him.

New Meaning

What would it be like for you and me if everything seemed new to us? It is a puzzling question, isn't it?

When Our Lady held her child in her arms, she must have had this sense of 'everything seeming new' to her. God had broken into her life and become its Centre. Everything seems new when that happens: a God-event is what brings about the change. The world could seem the same as before, but now that God has entered it, everything is fresh and surprising and has a new meaning. There is nothing boring about any aspect of human life. 'The earth is charged with the grandeur of God' (G. M. Hopkins). Humankind is, as it were, 'plugged into God':

the divine current is energising every detail of human life from conception to death and into the fullness of eternal life. Because of the Incarnation, God can be sought and found in all human things. Ordinary matters matter infinitely!

All Unique

Can we find the extraordinary hidden behind the ordinary in our own lives? To her neighbours in Nazareth Mary looked like a very ordinary mother, but something extraordinary was going on in her life. Now the temptation we have is to think that she was extraordinarily graced and that the rest of us are not: the truth is that while Mary has a totally unique and intimate relationship with God, God never intended it to create an unbridgeable distance between herself and us. The world is not divided between those who are highly favoured by God and those who are not! Mary would want to say to any mother, 'Please don't distance me! Indeed, I am unique and have been specially graced, and my child is the chosen one of God. But you, too, are unique: you are specially graced, and your child is a chosen one of God also. As I see it, every one of us in the world is singled out for special attention by God and given - if we can receive it - everything we need for a special role which no one else can play. Let me walk side-by-side with you and let me support you as you journey along on the path of your own uniqueness.'

What, Me Special?

Ignatius describes his experience at Manresa as one in which everything seemed new to him. But the primary thing that was new was his appreciation of himself. Where before he thought of himself, and was seen by others, as a worldly man, obsessed with a desire for personal honour and glory, now 'it seemed to him that he was a different man and that he had a different intellect from the one he had before.' Ignatius doesn't tell us exactly what the difference was, but it's as if the blindness which afflicts us all was removed from him, so that he saw how close God was to him, how deeply God loved him, wanted him, and gifted him.

Awakening The Divinity Within

It's as if he had some breath-taking glimpse of the mystery of divinity within himself and then in all things human and in the material world. But the gift given to Ignatius is always being offered to us. God is not hiding it from us. It is waiting to be discovered. Frail and limited and sinful though we may be, all of us are in the process of becoming and being revealed as the daughters and sons of God and everything good in the world is provided for us, while everything that is not good is being worked on by God and turned towards our ultimate good. I am totally loved and God is looking after me in every possible way, and so I can rightly spend my life in seeking and finding God in everything.

Transformation

A suitable conclusion to this book is to indicate the changes that occurred in Ignatius' way of seeing things which enabled him to grow in his capacity to find God in everything.

The younger Ignatius is obsessed with a desire for worldly honours and glory: the mature Ignatius lives only for the honour and glory of God and finds himself directed to the poor and marginalised.

Where before he is ready to kill another person if honour requires it, later he wants only 'to help others' in every way he can. He will no longer use arms to sort out problems between people: instead, he will use the weapons of reverence, listening, helpful teaching, and encouragement: intractable situations he can now respectfully leave to God.

In the early stages of his conversion, he tries to storm heaven by excessive penances, and then by residing in the Holy Land. Later he learns not to run ahead of God nor to spoil God's work of art, and to recognise that every place is a holy place, because God is already there.

Private love affairs yield place to a love affair with God and a boundless love for all God's people. He learns that all human loves are good when set within divine love. His interest shifts from the endless wrangling of local lords to the universal concern of the 'eternal Lord of all things.'

Until his middle years he makes decisions to please himself, but gradually his life is taken over by Another and he becomes a person who wants to be open only to what might please God. He shifts from trying to do great things for God by individual effort to labouring with God and in companionship.

One could go on and on highlighting the changes that characterised Ignatius' inner pilgrimage from his own small, self-centred world to the limitless world whose centre is God. But the real point is for us to allow God to lead us, with whatever help Ignatius can offer, along the same pilgrimage and to the same destination, so that we, like Ignatius, come to see everything in a new way. Our tiny planet, wending its way among the stars, needs people who love it and its precious inhabitants 'in a different way', which is the way of God.

Christmas encapsulates all that God has in store for us - a human being is divine: God is fully present in a human being and desires to be fully present in each one of us.

May you experience 'the love that is beyond all telling' and may that gift blossom in responding love!

SUGGESTED EXERCISE

● 'I have a gift for you. I hope it will bring you joy.'

● How many times have we heard or spoken words like these?

● When you next sit with Jesus, look at the world together with him. Look at all the gifts that are present in our world - people, nature, places, sciences, skills.

● Invite Jesus to help you notice the gifts you have been given by God, the gifts which were and are given to you alone. The list might be surprising and long! Don't interrupt him! Simply be grateful.

● Before saying 'Goodbye' see yourself as a gift to God's world. Your prayer can be simple: 'Please show me how to be a gift to others. Help me to see.'

Trains

www.omio.co.uk

www.thetrainline.com

Buses

Stagecoach operates buses in Winchester and the surrounding area

www.stagecoachbus.com

Park & Ride

For information on car parks and timetables for the Park & Ride visit

www.winchester.gov.uk/parking/park-and-ride

Printed in Turkey by Pelikan Bassim using responsibly sourced paper.
A catalogue record for this book is available from the British Library.
© Crown copyright 2023 OS PU100012932
All photographs are by the author unless otherwise stated.

Acknowledgements
Thank you to my wife Patsie for her patience and support in getting me across the finishing line. I'm also very grateful to Tom Nixon and Anna, without whose technical help this guidebook would have simply remained an idea!

Updates to this Guide

While every effort is made to ensure the accuracy of guidebooks as they go to print, changes can occur during the lifetime of an edition. Any updates that we know of for this guide will be on the Cicerone website (www.cicerone.co.uk/1164/updates), so please check before planning your trip. We also advise that you check information about transport, accommodation and shops locally. We are always grateful for updates, sent by email to updates@cicerone.co.uk or by post to Cicerone, Juniper House, Murley Moss, Oxenholme Road, Kendal, LA9 7RL.

Register your book: To sign up to receive free updates, special offers and GPX files where available, register your book at www.cicerone.co.uk.